1God

prayers and proverbs to connect you with Him

by
Dr. Josie Washington Carr, Ed.D.

The Lord God hath given me the tongue of the
learned, that I should know how to speak a word in
season...he wakeneth mine ear to hear as the learned.

Isaiah 50:4

Harrison House
Tulsa, Oklahoma

18 17 16 15 14   10 9 8 7 6 5 4

iGod
prayers and proverbs to connect you with Him
ISBN 13: 978-1-57794-885-8
ISBN 10: 1-57794-885-8
Copyright © 2008 by Jostan Publications, Inc.
P.O. Box 672514
Houston, Texas 77267

Published by Harrison House, Inc.
P.O. Box 35035
Tulsa, Oklahoma 74153

> Dedication

This book is dedicated to:

> My loving mother, Mildred Irvin, who taught me to trust God, no matter what, and to pray everyday because *"prayer changes things."*

> My parents-in-love, Jackie and Gladys Carr, who love me as their very own.

> My husband, Dr. Stanley B. Carr, who continues to prove his love for me and his belief in me.

> My children, Jarvis and Jakia Carr, who are like olive vines round about my table and the reasons for this book.

> My sisters: Mary Truehill, Lilly Washington, Dianna Myles, and Cynthia Ellioe; and brothers: Kevin Washington, Calvin Washington, and Kenneth Norwood.

> My pastors, Drs. I.V. and Bridget Hilliard, who teach me the uncompromising Word of God.

> My friends and traveling buddies, Patrice Mayes, Beverly Newsome, and Ann Wilson.

> My professors at Texas Southern University who refused to give up on me.

> My teachers, family, and friends in Donaldsonville, Louisiana.

> And to all educators with whom God has allowed me to work and supervise. You have proven, with a vision and a committed team, God can and will do the impossible in the lives of students.

> Special Acknowledgements

Everything I have accomplished in this life has been done with the assistance of others. I want to express my sincere gratitude to several people without whose help this book would have remained only a thought.

Special thanks to my pastor, Dr. I.V. Hilliard, whose teaching has changed my life and to my first lady, Dr. Bridget Hilliard, who taught me how to pray and confess the Word of God over my situations. Thank you for believing in me. Because of the awesome impact you have made in my life, students, parents, and educators are being blessed all over the world.

I want to give a super-duper thanks to Pastor Sheldon Reed, who assisted me by willingly sharing his wisdom and recollection of Scriptures' content and meaning. Your encouragement has blessed my life.

A loving thanks to my staff—pastors Reginald Petitt, Derrell Foster, Thomas Foster, James Mitchell, Earline Pruitt, Brenda Mitchell, Laura Mitchell, Beverly Burkett, Denise Collie, Chester Jenkins, and Filecha Lucas—for your commitment to excellence, teamwork, and professionalism. You are a source of inspiration to me.

Thanks to Filecha Lucas, Hazel Hughes, and Ron Marshall for your assistance in bringing this project to completion.

> Table of Contents

> Introduction

This book was written to help you connect with
God, especially in the years of your education.
Whether in high school, college, adult education, or
vocational training, these prayers, insights, and
confessions will help you to persevere to the
completion of your desired goal.

I believe the platform of knowledge is the Word of
God. It is from the basis of this foundation that
every issue concerning life is addressed, corrected,
shuffled, modified, enhanced, or eliminated.

The Word tells us to imitate God as dear children.
According to Hebrews 11:3, "The worlds were
framed by the word of God." He spoke His world
into existence; and if we are to imitate Him, we
must do likewise. Romans 10: 9-10 tells us to believe
in our heart and confess with our mouth. It goes on
to say, "Confession is made unto...." Mark 11:23 tells
us that we will have what we say. We must download
what the Word of God says about us and confess or

speak that Word with our mouths. God WILL watch over His Word to perform it in our lives.

It is my desire for you to stand firm on the Word of God and overcome every hindering force that would attempt to derail your destiny.

I believe *prayer* is vital for success in every area of a Christian's life. As we look into the basic instruction book for living on earth (the Bible), we find it to be the cornerstone in the lives of Jesus and the apostles.

Paul spent many hours interceding for new believers. In Ephesians 1:16 he wrote, "[I] cease not to give thanks for you, making mention of you in my prayers." In Colossians 1:3 he said, "We give thanks to God and the Father of our Lord Jesus Christ, praying always for you." Luke 18:1 says, "Men ought always to pray, and not to faint." Prayer is the code to overcoming life's situations. It is the energy that starts up and maintains the passion to persevere and win.

According to 1 Corinthians 1: 4-9, God does not want you to lack in any area of your life. "I thank my God always on your behalf, for the grace of God

which is given you by Jesus Christ; that in every thing ye are enriched by him, in all utterance, and in all knowledge; even as the testimony of Christ was confirmed in you: so that ye come behind in no gift; waiting for the coming of our Lord Jesus Christ: who shall also confirm you unto the end, that ye may be blameless in the day of our Lord Jesus Christ. God is faithful, by whom ye were called unto the fellowship of his Son Jesus Christ our Lord."

God always answers prayer in the affirmative when it is based on His Word. He told us to "put Him in remembrance," or play back His Word. I John 5:14-15 tells us when we pray or ask anything according to God's will, we can have confidence that He has heard us and we have the petitions that we desire of Him. Jeremiah 1:12 says God will hasten His Word to perform it. God's Word is the answer to your problem.

This book contains prayers and confessions (declarations of faith) based on the Word of God that will bring victory to your situation. Sync with the Scriptures that have been provided for easy reference and deeper study.

prayers

to connect you with Him

Intelligent children make their parents proud;
lazy students embarrass their parents.

Proverbs 15:20 MESSAGE

> Daily Connection Prayer

Dear Father God,

Thank You for the opportunity to pray and receive the petitions I desire of You. What a privilege to be saved and standing in the righteousness of God through Christ Jesus! Thank You for all the benefits of my salvation that include peace, protection, and provision.

Father, I commit my works unto You, my thoughts are established and I have success in every area of my life. I pray and believe that my steps are ordered by You and You are delighting in my way.

According to Your Word, I ask You for wisdom for my education—every assignment and test. I receive and confess I have wisdom, now. Thank You for Jesus, who has been made wisdom unto me; and just as He increased in wisdom, so do I.

I acknowledge the Holy Spirit as my helper, teacher, guide, and comforter. Holy Spirit, You are welcome in every situation of my life. Thank You for teaching me all things and bringing to my remembrance, especially what I have studied. Because I am righteous, I

study how to answer on every assignment, quiz, and test. I have perfect recall!

I believe and confess that I am the head and not the tail, above only and not beneath. I am wiser than the children of the world and I am disciplined to do what is necessary to succeed in every task.

Thank You for my teachers and mentors whom You have sent to pour into my life the knowledge and skills necessary for my success in the earth.

Father, as I go through this day, I am confident in knowing I am complete in You, You are my helper, and I can do all things through Christ who gives me the strength. I cast all my cares on You because You care for me. In Jesus' name, **Amen.**

> Scripture Sync

And this is the confidence that we have in him, that, if we ask any thing according to his will, he heareth us: and if we know that he hear us, whatsoever we ask, we know that we have the petitions that we desired of him.   *I John 5:14-15*

3

For he hath made him to be sin for us, who knew no sin; that we might be made the righteousness of God in him.

2 Corinthians 5:21

Commit thy works unto the Lord, and thy thoughts shall be established. *Proverbs 16:3*

The steps of a good man are ordered by the Lord: and he delighteth in his way. *Psalm 37:23*

If any of you lack wisdom, let him ask of God, that giveth to all men liberally, and upbraideth not; and it shall be given him. *James 1:5*

And Jesus increased in wisdom and stature, and in favour with God and man. *Luke 2:52*

Behold, God is mine helper. *Psalm 54:4*

So that we may boldly say, The Lord is my helper, and I will not fear what man shall do unto me. *Hebrews 13:6*

But the Comforter (Counselor, Helper, Intercessor, Advocate, Strengthener, Standby), the Holy Spirit, Whom the Father will send in My name [in My place, to represent Me and act on My behalf], He will teach you all things. And He will cause you to recall (will remind you of, bring to your remembrance) everything I have told you.

John 14:26 AMP

The heart of the righteous studieth to answer: but the mouth of the wicked poureth out evil things. *Proverbs 15:28*

4

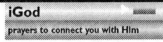

And the Lord shall make you the head, and not the tail;
and you shall be above only, and you shall not be beneath,
if you heed the commandments of the Lord your God
which I command you this day and are watchful to do
them.   *Deuteronomy 28:13* AMP

We have boldness and access with confidence by the faith
of him.   *Ephesians 3:12*

And ye are complete in him, which is the head of all prin-
cipality and power.   *Colossians 2:10*

I can do all things through Christ which strengtheneth me.
                                      Philippians 4:13

Cast all your care upon him; for he careth for you.
                                      I Peter 5:7

iGod
prayers to connect you with Him   >

> Prayer for Academic Excellence

This is the day that the Lord has made,
I choose to rejoice and be glad in it. Father, I pause
to give You thanks for who You are in my life.

As I start this day, I declare I am a disciple taught of
the Lord and obedient to Your will. Great is my
peace and undisturbed composure.

I choose to obey Your Word and to submit to those
in authority over me. I choose to respect my parents
and teachers. I use wisdom and make the right
choices in every situation. I speak only that which is
good and beneficial. I please You with my thoughts,
words, and actions as I walk in integrity of heart.

Thank You, Father, that I have the mind to stay
focused in all my academic endeavors. I am ten times
wiser than the children of the world. I am the head
and not the tail. I am above only and not beneath,
blessed coming in and going out.

I pray and confess that I find favor, good understanding, and high esteem with God, my parents, my

6

classmates, and my teachers. I cultivate an apprecia-
tion for education and living a life that is pleasing
to God. In Jesus' name, **Amen.**

> Scripture Sync

This is the day which the Lord hath made; we will rejoice
and be glad in it.   *Psalm 118:24*

And all thy children shall be taught of the Lord; and great
shall be the peace of thy children.   *Isaiah 54:13*

Children, obey your parents in the Lord: for this is right.
Honour thy father and mother; which is the first commandment with promise; that it may be well with thee, and thou
mayest live long on the earth.   *Ephesians 6:1-3*

And in all matters of wisdom and understanding, that the
king enquired of them, he found them ten times better
than all the magicians and astrologers that were in all his
realm.   *Daniel 1:20*

And Jesus increased in wisdom and stature, and in favour
with God and man.   *Luke 2:52*

> Prayer When Experiencing Anger

Father, I am Your child and I choose to put aside all anger and strife. God, I speak peace to the raging thoughts that may flood my mind. Devil, I command you to take your hands off me; I am set apart for the work of God. Anger, you will not destroy me. I am the seed of the righteous and I am delivered from every trick of the devil.

Father, because You promised that You would never break Your covenant, nor alter the thing that has gone out of Your lips, I pray and believe that I operate in the peace of God that surpasses all understanding and keeps my heart and mind quiet through Christ Jesus. I declare, the peace of God and a calm spirit overshadow me in every situation, and cause me to act accordingly.

I confess I am kind to everyone. I am tenderhearted, willing to forgive others just as God has forgiven me. I make the quality decision to put aside all bitterness, wrath, anger, uproar, and evil speaking. I believe, therefore I say, I am swift to hear, slow to

speak, and slow to wrath so that the light of Jesus
will shine upon my path.

Father, I see myself as a student of great peace,
purpose, and productivity. In Jesus' name, **Amen.**

> Scripture Sync

Let no corrupt communication proceed out of your
mouth, but that which is good to the use of edifying that it
may minister grace unto the hearers. And grieve not the
holy Spirit of God, whereby ye are sealed unto the day of
redemption. Let all bitterness, and wrath, and anger, and
clamour, and evil speaking, be put away from you, with all
malice: and be ye kind one to another, tenderhearted,
forgiving one another, even as God for Christ's sake hath
forgiven you.   *Ephesians 4:29-32*

Wherefore, my beloved brethren, let every man be swift
to hear, slow to speak, slow to wrath.   *James 1:19*

He that is slow to wrath is of great understanding: but he
that is hasty of spirit exalteth folly.   *Proverbs 14:29*

A wrathful man stirreth up strife: but he that is slow to
anger appeaseth strife.   *Proverbs 15:18*

He that is slow to anger is better than the mighty; and he that
ruleth his spirit than he that taketh a city.   *Proverbs 16:32*

> Prayer for Confidence

Father, in the name of Jesus, I come before You in faith, praising and thanking You for Your faithfulness to confirm Your Word with signs following.

I believe and confess I approach each day and assignment with confidence, knowing that You have begun a good work in me and will perform it until the day of Jesus Christ. I boldly declare You as my helper and I choose not to fear or be terrified of anything. I know that success is not merely achieved by my might nor by my power, but by Your spirit working in and through me.

Father, thank You that there is nothing too hard for You. Even when it seems there is no way out of my situation, I rejoice, knowing You always cause me to triumph in Christ Jesus. I confidently say, You are my strength and You will make my feet like hinds' feet and cause me to walk upon high places. In Jesus' name, **Amen.**

> Scripture Sync

And they went forth, and preached every where, the Lord working with them, and confirming the word with signs following. Amen. *Mark 16:20*

Being confident of this very thing, that he which hath begun a good work in you will perform it until the day of Jesus Christ. *Philippians 1:6*

Then he answered and spake unto me, saying, This is the word of the Lord unto Zerubbabel, saying, Not by might, nor by power, but by my spirit, saith the Lord of hosts. *Zechariah 4:6*

Now thanks be unto God, which always causeth me to triumph in Christ, and maketh manifest the savour of his knowledge by us in every place. *2 Corinthians 2:14*

Ah Lord God! behold, thou hast made the heaven and the earth by thy great power and stretched out arm, and there is nothing too hard for thee. *Jeremiah 32:17*

The Lord God is my strength, and he will make my feet like hinds' feet, and he will make me to walk upon mine high places. *Habakkuk 3:19*

> Prayer for Discipline

Father, in the name of Jesus, I pray and confess Your Word today concerning discipline in my life. I know when I pray according to Your Word, You hear me and grant the petitions that I desire of You. Thank You for being a faithful God.

Your Word says that faith, without the implementation of works, is dead; therefore, I believe I have the discipline to read, study, and complete all assignments in a timely manner. I realize this does not make me a weak person, but, according to Your Word, it causes me to increase in strength. Help me to cultivate and meditate upon these duties and throw myself wholly into them so that my progress may appear to all.

Father, I pray as I develop in knowledge, I also develop in self-control and endurance. I confess I am a disciplined person, obedient to Your Word, and I have great peace and success. In Jesus' name, **Amen.**

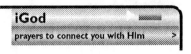
> Scripture Sync

Then said the Lord to me, You have seen well, for I am
alert and active, watching over My word to perform it.
Jeremiah 1:12 AMP

God is faithful (reliable, trustworthy, and therefore ever
true to His promise, and He can be depended on); by Him
you were called into companionship and participation with
His Son, Jesus Christ our Lord.   *1 Corinthians 1:9* AMP

A wise man is strong; yea, a man of knowledge increaseth
strength.   *Proverbs 24:5*

Practice and cultivate and meditate upon these duties; throw
yourself wholly into them [as your ministry], so that your
progress may be evident to everybody.   *1 Timothy 4:15* AMP

And all your [spiritual] children shall be disciples [taught
by the Lord and obedient to His will], and great shall be
the peace and undisturbed composure of your children.
Isaiah 54:13 AMP

For this very reason, adding your diligence [to the divine
promises], employ every effort in exercising your faith to
develop virtue (excellence, resolution, Christian energy),
and in [exercising] virtue [develop] knowledge (intelli-
gence).   *2 Peter 1:5* AMP

13

> Prayer for Employment

Father, in the name of Jesus, You are my rock and fortress; therefore, for Your name's sake, lead and guide me. I choose not to fear because You are with me. You are the Lord, my God, who teaches me to profit and leads me in the way I should go.

As I prepare and seek employment, I ask You to move on the hearts of the people responsible for making employment decisions. I believe their hearts are in Your hand and You are turning them towards me. Your Word says promotion comes from You. You put down one and set up another. Thank You for setting me in my desired position with my desired salary, knowing that You always do exceeding abundantly above all I ask or think.

Your Word declares that in all labor there is profit; therefore, I commit my work unto You. You establish my thoughts and cause my plans to succeed. According to Your Word, I believe and say, You have made me the head and not the tail, above only and not beneath. To God be all the glory! In Jesus' name, **Amen.**

> Scripture Sync

For thou art my rock and my fortress; therefore for thy name's sake lead me, and guide me. *Psalm 31:3*

Fear thou not; for I am with thee: be not dismayed; for I am thy God: I will strengthen thee; yea, I will help thee; yea, I will uphold thee with the right hand of my righteousness. *Isaiah 41:10*

Thus saith the Lord, thy Redeemer, the Holy One of Israel; I am the Lord thy God which teacheth thee to profit, which leadeth thee by the way that thou shouldest go. *Isaiah 48:17*

The king's heart is in the hand of the Lord, as the rivers of water: he turneth it whithersoever he will. *Proverbs 21:1*

For promotion cometh neither from the east, nor from the west, nor from the south. But God is the judge: he putteth down one, and setteth up another.

Psalm 75:6-7

Roll your works upon the Lord (commit and trust them wholly to Him; He will cause your thoughts to become agreeable to His will, and) so shall your plans be established and succeed. *Proverbs 16:3 AMP*

And the Lord shall make you the head, and not the tail; and you shall be above only, and you shall not be beneath, if you heed the commandments of the Lord your God

15

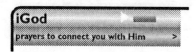

which I command you this day and are watchful to do
them. *Deuteronomy 28:13 AMP*

God so loved the world, that he gave his only begotten
Son. *John 3:16*

Wisely train the young women to be sane and sober of
mind (temperate, disciplined) and to love their husbands
and their children. *Titus 2:4 AMP*

Love one another with brotherly affection [as members of
one family], giving precedence and showing honor to one
another. *Romans 12:10 AMP*

16

> Prayer When Experiencing Fear

Dear God, what a privilege to come before Your throne of grace. Father, You are love and You are perfect. Thank You that perfect love casts out all fear; and because of that perfect love I choose not to fear, nor allow my heart to be troubled or afraid. There is no fear in love, and You have not given me a spirit of fear, but of power, love, and a sound mind.

I speak to the forces of darkness in the mighty name of Jesus! I call your assignment of fear to naught against me and I command you to take your hands off me because I am God's property. I plead the blood of Jesus over me and declare no evil shall come nigh me or nigh my dwelling. God has given His angels charge over me and the angels will keep me safe in all my ways.

Father, I am grateful for Your unconditional love that overshadows me; therefore, I boldly say, "The Lord is my helper; I will not fear, what can man do to me?" I approach every assignment and endeavor

17

with confidence, which will cause my grades, class-room participation, and conduct to excel.

Thank You, Father, that I see myself functioning in the peace of God as I become the person of purpose and great productivity that You have called me to be. In Jesus' name, **Amen.**

> Scripture Sync

For God hath not given us the spirit of fear; but of power, and of love, and of a sound mind.   *2 Timothy 1:7*

There is no fear in love; but perfect love casteth out fear: because fear hath torment. He that feareth is not made perfect in love.   *1 John 4:18*

There shall no evil befall thee, neither shall any plague come nigh thy dwelling. For he shall give his angels charge over thee, to keep thee in all thy ways.   *Psalm 91: 10-11*

The Lord is on my side; I will not fear: what can man do unto me?   *Psalm 118:6*

The Lord is my light and salvation; whom shall I fear? the Lord is the strength of my life; of whom shall I be afraid? Though an host should encamp against me, my heart shall not fear: though war should rise against me, in this will I be confident.   *Psalm 27:1,3*

> Prayer for Finances

Father, in the name of Jesus, thank You for Your Word that will not return void but accomplishes what it says and prospers in the situation in which I send it.

I confess Your Word with my mouth and believe in my heart that because I honor You with my tithe and offering, I experience the windows of heaven's blessings (favor, insight, and financial increase) in my life. I believe every need is met with heaven's best. And because You have given me everything that pertains to life and godliness, I confess my tuition, books, housing, and everything concerning school is paid in full.

I will not take a (worrying) thought by saying, "How can I ever pay for_____." I will continue to seek first the kingdom of God, and those things will be added to me. I declare, I will not lack any beneficial thing. In Jesus' name, **Amen.**

19

> Scripture Sync

So shall my word be that goeth forth out of my mouth: it shall not return unto me void, but it shall accomplish that which I please, and it shall prosper in the thing whereto I sent it. *Isaiah 55:11*

Bring ye all the tithes into the storehouse, that there may be meat in mine house, and prove me now herewith, saith the Lord of hosts, if I will not open you the windows of heaven, and pour you out a blessing, that there shall not be room enough to receive it. *Malachi 3:10*

But my God shall supply all your need according to his riches in glory by Christ Jesus. *Philippians 4:19*

According as his divine power hath given unto us all things that pertain unto life and godliness, through the knowledge of him that hath called us to glory and virtue.

2 Peter 1:3

Therefore take no thought, saying, What shall we eat? or, What shall we drink? or, Wherewithal shall we be clothed? (For after all these things do the Gentiles seek:) for your heavenly Father knoweth that ye have need of all these things. But seek ye first the kingdom of God, and his righteousness; and all these things shall be added unto you.

Matthew 6:31-33

> Prayer for Graduation

Praise the name of the Lord, for Your name is excellent; Your glory is above the heavens. Thank You for Your Word that says to call unto You and You will show me great and mighty things I know not. Through You, I have done valiantly, and You have treaded down every enemy that came against me.

As I approach graduation day, thank You for every need being met with heaven's best and for giving me my expected end. Thank You for my parents, family, and friends who supported me through this endeavor. I speak choice blessings on them; and because they helped to bring my dream to pass, I know You will cause the same to happen for them.

As I move forward, thank You for Your favor that surrounds me as a shield. My steps are ordered by You and I believe You have raised up someone to use his/her power, ability, and influence to help me. I pray and believe You will instruct, guide, and teach me in the way I should go.

21

iGod

prayers to connect you with Him >

Father, thank You for perfecting everything that concerns me. In Jesus' name, **Amen.**

> Scripture Sync

Call unto me, and I will answer thee, and show thee great and mighty things, which thou knowest not.

Jeremiah 33:3

Through God we shall do valiantly: for he it is that shall tread down our enemies. *Psalm 60:12*

For I know the thoughts that I think toward you, saith the Lord, thoughts of peace, and not of evil, to give you an expected end. *Jeremiah 29:11*

Whatsoever good thing any man doeth, the same shall he receive of the Lord. *Ephesians 6:8*

The steps of a good man are ordered by the Lord: and he delighteth in his way. *Psalm 37:23*

And God is able to make all grace (*favor*) abound toward you; that ye, always having all sufficiency in all things, may abound to every good work. *2 Corinthians 9:8*

I will instruct thee and teach thee in the way which thou shalt go: I will guide thee with mine eye. *Psalm 32:8*

> Prayer When Experiencing Grief

Father, in the name of Jesus, I thank You for being my very present help and for delivering me out of all my troubles. Your Word declares Jesus has already borne my sorrows and grief; therefore, I believe and confess that I am free and experiencing the peace of God during this time of loss.

Father, Psalm 107:20 says that You sent Your Word and healed and delivered Your people from destruction. I receive that Word and declare that I am healed, delivered, and set free from sickness, sorrow, grief, pain, and destruction. I have confidence that the Word will not return void but it will accomplish the desired objective.

Spirit of sorrow, in the name of Jesus, go now! Spirit of grief, in the name of Jesus, go now! Spirits of sickness, disease, and destruction, I command you to go now. I take authority over you and declare you can no longer harass me. In Jesus' name, I call your assignment to naught. I am free to learn and participate at school. I am free to enjoy my family, at

23

home. I am free to participate at church and in leisure activities.

Father, according to Your Word, I confess that I shall return to school with singing, joy, and gladness because sorrow has fled away. I choose to think on things that are true, honest, pure, and of good report, as I am strengthened by the joy of the Lord.

Holy Spirit, I welcome You into this situation. Thank You for comforting, leading, and guiding me. I am the redeemed of the Lord and I declare that I am a person of divine purpose and great productivity. In Jesus' name, **Amen.**

iGod

prayers to connect you with Him >

> Scripture Sync

Surely he hath borne our griefs, and carried our sorrows: yet we did esteem him stricken, smitten of God, and afflicted. *Isaiah 53:4*

Then he said unto them, Go your way, eat the fat, and drink the sweet, and send portions unto them for whom nothing is prepared: for this day is holy unto our Lord: neither be ye sorry; for the joy of the Lord is your strength. *Nehemiah 8:10*

He sent His word and healed them, and delivered them from their destructions. *Psalm 107:20*

Verily, verily, I say unto you, He that believeth on me, the works that I do shall he do also; and greater works than these shall he do; because I go unto my Father.

John 14:12

> Prayer When Experiencing a Health Challenge

Father, in Jesus' name, I believe that I am healed by the stripes of Jesus. Jesus bore my sickness on the tree, and with boldness I command sickness to flee my body! Every symptom must cease and leave my body now in the name of Jesus.

Father, I thank You that Your Word is medicine to my body and life to my flesh. I see myself walking in divine health all the days of my life.

I speak Your Word that says You heal all our diseases. I boldly declare that I shall live and not die and declare the works of the Lord. I believe my health is springing forth speedily and I will continue to be a person of divine purpose and great productivity. In the name of Jesus, **Amen.**

> Scripture Sync

Who his own self bare our sins in his own body on the tree, that we, being dead to sins, should live unto right-eousness: by whose stripes ye were healed.

1 Peter 2:24

My son, attend to my words; incline thine ear unto my sayings. Let them not depart from thine eyes; keep them in the midst of thine heart. For they are life unto those that find them, and health to all their flesh. Keep thy heart with all diligence; for out of it are the issues of life.

Proverbs 4:20-23

Bless the Lord, O my soul, and forget not all his benefits: who forgiveth all thine iniquities; who healeth all thy diseases. *Psalm 103:2-3*

Because thou hast made the Lord, which is my refuge, even the most High, thy habitation; there shall no evil befall thee, neither shall any plague come nigh thy dwelling. *Psalm 91:9-10*

> Prayer for Recovery After Making a Mistake

Father, I acknowledge and confess that I sinned against You and _____ when I did _____. Thank You for Your Word that declares I can confess my sin and You are faithful to forgive me and cleanse me from all unrighteousness. Thank You for forgiving and cleansing me; therefore, I am in right standing with You. According to Your Word in Romans 8:1, I have no condemnation because I am in Christ Jesus and live according to the dictates of the Spirit.

I now plead the blood of Jesus over my mind regarding this matter. I renounce any harm, ill-feeling, or disadvantage this may have caused to others. Thank You for the comforting ministry of the Holy Spirit on their behalf—as well as mine—as I continue to walk, looking only unto Jesus, who is the author and finisher of my faith.

It is my desire to please You with my life; therefore, I ask You to create in me a clean heart and renew a right spirit within me. Restore unto me the joy of

28

my salvation and uphold me with Your free spirit. In Jesus' name, **Amen.**

> Scripture Sync

If we confess our sins, he is faithful and just to forgive us our sins, and to cleanse us from all unrighteousness.

1 John 1:9

Create in me a clean heart, O God; and renew a right spirit within me. Restore unto me the joy of thy salvation; and uphold me with thy free spirit. Then will I teach transgressors thy ways; and sinners shall be converted unto thee. *Psalm 51:10,12-13*

Looking unto Jesus the author and finisher of our faith....

Hebrews 12:2

> Prayer for Perseverance

Glory to God in the highest! Thank You for the privilege and opportunity to pray Your Word with the assurance that You will grant the things I desire of You.

Father, I am standing on Your Word that declares You are my very present help, strength, refuge, and fortress. You have already delivered me and You always cause me to win in Christ Jesus.

Thank You for helping me to persevere. I realize, through faith and patience, I will attain my goal. I hold fast to my confession of faith without wavering because You are faithful who promised.

Father, I believe the work that You have begun in me, You will continue to completion; therefore, I forget those things that are behind (failures, mistakes) and press toward the prize. In Jesus' name, **Amen.**

> Scripture Sync

The Lord God is my strength.   *Habakkuk 3:19*

I will say of the Lord, He is my refuge and my fortress: my God; in him will I trust.   *Psalm 91:2*

Now thanks be unto God, which always causeth us to triumph in Christ, and maketh manifest the savour of his knowledge by us in every place.   *2 Corinthians 2:14*

Let us hold fast the profession of our faith without wavering; (for he is faithful that promised).   *Hebrews 10:23*

Brethen, I count not myself to have apprehended: but this one thing I do, forgetting those things which are behind, and reaching forth unto those things which are before, I press toward the mark for the prize of the high calling of God in Christ Jesus.   *Philippians 3:13-14*

The hand of the diligent shall bear rule: but the slothful shall be under tribute.   *Proverbs 12:24*

He becometh poor that dealeth with a slack hand: but the hand of the diligent maketh rich.   *Proverbs 10:4*

> Prayer for Promotion

Father, in Jesus' name, Your Word says promotions do not come from the east, nor the west, nor the south; but God is the judge who puts down one and picks up another.

I believe You perfect everything that concerns me. Therefore, according to Your Word, You are elevating me to the next level in _____. Father, You are my very present help in times when I do not know what to do. Thank You for showering me with Your favor as I operate in faithfulness and integrity regarding my situation.

Thank You for raising up someone, somewhere, to use his/her power, ability, and influence to help me, and for the wisdom necessary to complete all that has been assigned to me.

I live in daily expectation of my promotion. In Jesus' name, **Amen!**

> Scripture Sync

For promotion cometh neither from the east, nor from the west, nor from the south. But God is the judge: he putteth down one, and setteth up another.

Psalm 75:6,7

The Lord will perfect that which concerneth me: thy mercy, O Lord, endureth for ever: forsake not the works of thine own hands.   *Psalm 138:8*

If any of you lack wisdom, let him ask of God, that giveth to all men liberally, and upbraideth not; and it shall be given him.   *James 1:5*

And God is able to make all grace abound toward you; that ye, always having all sufficiency in all things, may abound to every good work.   *2 Corinthians 9:8*

> Prayer Against Rebellion

Father, in Jesus' name, I speak Your word over me concerning a rebellious attitude. I pray, believe, and confess that I am submitted to God. I resist the devil, and he flees from me.

Your Word declares that rebellion is as the sin of witchcraft and stubbornness is as iniquity and idolatry. Therefore, in the name of Jesus, I command the spirit of rebellion to leave me. I resist the temptation to rebel, in Jesus' name. I loose the spirit of obedience to overshadow my life. I pray and believe that I am protected by the blood of Jesus, delivered from the powers of darkness, and walking in the divine peace of God. I choose to be obedient and eat the good of the land and to obey and be submissive to those who are in authority over me and watch for my soul.

Lord, my heart is pure and I speak excellent and noble things regarding my situation. The opening of my lips shall be to speak the Word of God over my life, declaring that I am a student of excellence, great peace, and divine productivity. In Jesus' name, **Amen.**

34

> Scripture Sync

Submit yourselves therefore to God. Resist the devil, and
he will flee from you.   *James 4:7*

Though hand join in hand, the wicked shall not be unpun-
ished: but the seed of the righteous shall be delivered.
                                          Proverbs 11:21

If ye be willing and obedient, ye shall eat the good of the
land.   *Isaiah 1:19*

Verily I say unto you, Whatsoever ye shall bind on earth
shall be bound in heaven: and whatsoever ye shall loose
on earth shall be loosed in heaven. Again I say unto you,
That if two of you shall agree on earth as touching any
thing that they shall ask, it shall be done for them of my
Father which is in heaven.   *Matthew 18:18-19*

Obey them that have the rule over you, and submit yourselves: for they watch for your souls, as they that must
give account, that they may do it with joy, and not with
grief: for that is unprofitable for you.   *Hebrews 13:17*

Who hath delivered us from the power of darkness, and
hath translated us into the kingdom of his dear Son.
                                          Colossians 1:13

35

> Prayer to Receive the Rewards of Obedience

Father, thank You for Your Word that says:

- Obey your parents in the Lord: for this is right. Honor your father and mother which is the first commandment with promise; that it may be well with you, and that you may live long on the earth.

- Obey your parents in all things: for this is pleasing unto the Lord.

- Honor your father and your mother, as the Lord your God has commanded you; that your days may be prolonged, and that it may go well with you....

- Even a child is known by what he does, whether his work is pure, and whether it is right.

- Whoever keeps the law is a wise son: but he that is a companion of riotous people shames his father.

- Blessed are those that keep my ways. Hear instruction, and be wise, and refuse it not.

36

Your Word declares if I am willing and obedient, I
will eat the good of the land; but if I rebel, I will be
devoured by the sword. Father, I am willing, and I
choose to obey. In Jesus' name, **Amen.**

> Scripture Sync

Children, obey your parents in the Lord: for this is right.
Honour thy father and mother; which is the first commandment with promise; that it may be well with thee, and thou
mayest live long on the earth.   *Ephesians 6:1-3*

Children, obey your parents in all things: for this is well
pleasing unto the Lord.   *Colossians 3:20*

Honour thy father and thy mother, as the Lord thy God
hath commandeth thee; that thy days may be prolonged,
and that it may go well with thee.   *Deuteronomy 5:16*

Even a child is known by his doings, whether his work be
pure, and whether it be right.   *Proverbs 20:11*

Whoso keepeth the law is a wise son: but he that is a
companion of riotous men shameth his father.

Proverbs 28:7

If ye be willing and obedient, ye shall eat the good of the
land: but if ye refuse and rebel, ye shall be devoured with
the sword: for the mouth of the Lord hath spoken it.

Isaiah 1:19-20

> Prayer for Safety

Father, Your name is a strong tower; the righteous run into it and they are safe. Thank You for watching over Your Word to perform it in my life.

I pray, believe, and confess that I dwell in the secret place of the Most High and remain stable and fixed under the shadow of the Almighty, whose power no foe can withstand. I will say, You are my refuge, my fortress, and my God. I lean and rely on You. I confidently trust You. You have delivered me from the snare of the devil. Your truth and faithfulness are a shield and buckler for me. I choose not to fear the terror of the night, nor the arrows of the wicked that flies by day. A thousand may fall at my side and ten thousand at my right hand, but it shall not come near me. I will only be a spectator as I witness the reward of the wicked. I have made the Lord my refuge and the Most High my dwelling place; therefore, no evil shall befall me nor any plague come near my dwelling. You have given Your angels charge over me to accompany, defend, and preserve me in all my ways of service and obedience. I call upon You

and You answer me. You are with me when I am in trouble. You deliver me out of trouble and honor me. With long life You satisfy me and show me Your salvation. In Jesus' name, **Amen.**

> Scripture Sync

The name of the Lord is a strong tower: the righteous runneth into it, and is safe.   *Proverbs 18:10*

Then said the Lord into me, Thou hast well seen: for I will hasten my word to perform it.   *Jeremiah 1:12*

He that dwelleth in the secret place of the most High shall abide under the shadow of the Almighty. I will say of the Lord, He is my refuge and my fortress: my God; in him will I trust. Surely he shall deliver thee from the snare of the fowler, and from the noisome pestilence. He shall cover thee with his feathers, and under his wings shalt thou trust: his truth shall be thy shield and buckler. Thou shalt not be afraid for the terror by night; nor for the arrow that flieth by day; nor for the pestilence that walketh in darkness; nor for the destruction that wasteth at noonday. A thousand shall fall at thy side, and ten thousand at thy right hand; but it shall not come nigh thee. Only with thine eyes shalt thou behold and see the reward of the wicked. Because thou hast made the Lord,

which is my refuge, even the most High, thy habitation;
there shall no evil befall thee, neither shall any plague
come nigh thy dwelling. For he shall give his angels charge
over thee, to keep thee in all thy ways. They shall bear
thee up in their hands, lest thou dash thy foot against a
stone. Thou shalt tread upon the lion and adder: the
young lion and the dragon shalt thou trample under feet.
Because he hath set his love upon me, therefore will I
deliver him: I will set him on high, because he hath known
my name. He shall call upon me, and I will answer him: I
will be with him in trouble; I will deliver him, and honour
him. With long life will I satisfy him, and shew him my
salvation.   *Psalm 91:1-16*

You are my hiding place; you will protect me from trouble
and surround me with songs of deliverance.

                                              Psalm 32:7 NIV

> Prayer for Strong Self-Esteem

Father, in Jesus' name, I pray, believe, and confess that I am a disciple taught of the Lord, obedient to God's will, with great peace and undisturbed composure. I can do all things through Christ who strengthens me. I have the mind of Christ and hold the thoughts, feelings, and purposes of God's heart. I do not fret or have anxiety about anything.

The Word of God dwells richly in me, and He who has begun a good work in me will continue to perform it until the day of Jesus Christ. The joy of the Lord is my strength, and I am experiencing the peace of God in every situation of my life. I think on things that are true, honest, just, pure, lovely, and of a good report.

In all these things. We are more than conquerors.

Romans 8:37

I can do all things through Christ which strengtheneth me.

Philippians 4:13

Greater is he that is in [I] me, than he that is in the world.

I John 4:4

41

Forgetting those things which are behind...I press toward the mark for the prize of the high calling of God in Christ Jesus. *Philippians 3:13-14*

I see myself as God sees me, and I am a person of purpose and great productivity. In Jesus' name, **Amen.**

> Scripture Sync

And all thy children shall be taught of the Lord; and great shall be the peace of thy children. *Isaiah 54:13*

Be careful for nothing; but in every thing by prayer and supplication with thanksgiving let your requests be made known unto God. *Philippians 4:6*

Being confident of this very thing, that he which hath begun a good work in you will perform it until the day of Jesus Christ. *Philippians 1:6*

This day is holy unto our Lord: neither be ye sorry; for the joy of the Lord is your strength. *Nehemiah 8:10*

> Prayer to Walk in Love

Father, thank You for the love of God that has been shed abroad in my heart by the Holy Ghost. Help me to operate in that love with all my friends, classmates, and teachers. Your Word declares that perfect love casts out all fear. Therefore, I commit to walk in the God-kind of love. I am patient, kind, and endure long. I am not boastful, jealous, or envious. I am not self-seeking, fretful, or resentful. I choose to respect the rights and ways of others. I rejoice when truth prevails. My hopes and desires for others are fadeless under all circumstances. I overcome challenges without weakening, because love never fails.

I ask You to forgive those who persecute and mistreat me. I speak blessings on them and pray for opportunities to be a blessing to them. I pray and believe whenever I am in their presence, You will speak a word in due season to them that will cause victory to take place in their lives.

Father, because I am rooted and grounded in love, I believe You cause me to find favor, compassion, and

43

loving-kindness with my friends, family, school person-
nel, and others that I meet. In Jesus' name, **Amen.**

> Scripture Sync

But I say unto you, Love your enemies, bless them that
curse you, do good to them that hate you, and pray for
them which despitefully use you, and persecute you.

Matthew 5:44

Charity suffereth long, and is kind; charity envieth not;
charity vaunteth not itself, is not puffed up, doth not
behave itself unseemly, seeketh not her own, is not easily
provoked, thinketh no evil; rejoiceth not in iniquity, but
rejoiceth in the truth; beareth all things, believeth all
things, hopeth all things, endureth all things. Charity never
faileth: but whether there be prophecies, they shall fail;
whether there be tongues, they shall cease; whether there
be knowledge, it shall vanish away.   *1 Corinthians 13:4-8*

The wise in heart shall be called prudent: and the sweet-
ness of the lips increaseth learning.   *Proverbs 16:21*

now playing

Wisdom
From
Proverbs

> Wisdom From Proverbs

God wants us to live successful lives. He did not
create man to make him miserable. He created man
to connect with Him and have dominion in the
earth. God expects for us to rule over our situations and circumstances, not for them to rule us.

Life can, at times, be littered with unpleasant
encounters. If you do not know God, His ways, or
His Word, you may find yourself being overcome by
what you should be overcoming.

Experiencing good success in this life can only be
achieved through God's wisdom. Proverbs 4:7 tells
us that wisdom is the principle thing. Wisdom
teaches us God's ways and how to conduct
ourselves in compliance with His will.

Wisdom is found in the Word of God. The book of
Proverbs is known as the book of wisdom and was
written "That people may know skillful and godly
wisdom and instruction discern, and comprehend
the words of understanding and insight, receive
instruction in wise dealing and the discipline of wise

46

thoughtfulness, righteousness, justice, and integrity. That prudence may be given to the simple, and knowledge, discretion, and discernment to the youth. The wise also will hear and increase in learning, and the person of understanding will acquire skill and attain to sound counsel so that he may be able to steer his course rightly." (Proverbs 1:2-5 AMP)

It is important for believers to sync with the Word of God on a daily basis. Our natural man is fed daily and, in like manner, so should we feed our spirit man. Proverbs 4:20-22 talks about us giving attention to the Word and keeping it in the center of our hearts because it is life to us and medicine to our flesh.

Connecting with God through His Word is the spiritual panacea for the challenges of our schools and society. As a student you need to charge up daily by reading and confessing the Word of God. Then you will experience peace (beyond your current imagination), length of days, and divine health.

› The Reading Plan

The book of Proverbs has thirty-one chapters: a chapter for each day of the month. I recommend that you read chapter one on the first day of each month. On the second day of each month, read chapter two, and so on.

Confessions or declarations of faith from each chapter have been provided. Confess the Word, audibly. As you make these confessions out loud, they will reshape how you see yourself and you will become the confident, strong person that is mirrored in the Word of God. Remember Romans 10:9-10 says that confession is made unto (whatever you are confessing). For example, if you regularly confess that you have the peace of God, you will begin to operate in the peace of God.

Warning: You are about to experience an extreme upgrade by the power of God's Word. The following pages will change your life. Proceed with great expectation!

> Proverbs 1

Success

My son, hear the instruction of thy father, and forsake
not the law of thy mother: for they shall be an ornament
of grace unto thy head, and chains about thy neck.

Proverbs 1:8-9

Confess

I listen to the instruction of my father and receive the
teaching of my mother and it brings me grace and favor.

Protection

But whoso hearkeneth unto me shall dwell safely, and shall
be quiet from fear of evil.   *Proverbs 1:33*

Confess

I listen to wisdom and I live safely without fear.

> Proverbs 2

Success

My son, if thou wilt receive my words, and hide my
commandments with thee; so that thou incline thine ear
unto wisdom, and apply thine heart to understanding; yea,
if thou criest after knowledge, and liftest up thy voice for
understanding; if thou seekest her as silver, and searchest
for her as for hid treasures; then shalt thou understand

the fear of the Lord, and find the knowledge of God.

Proverbs 2:1-5

Confess

I receive the words of the Lord and store up His commands. I listen for His wisdom and apply it to my life. I seek God's counsel just like hidden treasure. I honor the Lord and find the knowledge of God.

Wisdom

When wisdom entereth into thine heart, and knowledge is pleasant unto thy soul; discretion shall preserve thee, understanding shall keep thee: to deliver thee from the way of the evil man, from the man that speaketh froward things.

Proverbs 2:10-12

Confess

I have wisdom, knowledge, discretion, and understanding; therefore, I am delivered from what people say and do.

Wisdom

Walk in the way of good men, and keep the paths of the righteous.

Proverbs 2:20

Confess

I walk in the path of the consistently righteous.

> Proverbs 3

Success

My son, forget not my law; but let thine heart keep my commandments: for length of days, and long life, and peace, shall they add to thee. *Proverbs 3:1-2*

Confess

I read, pray, meditate, and speak the Word of God and it adds length of days, long life, and peace unto me.

Favor

Let not mercy and truth forsake thee: bind them about thy neck; write them upon the table of thine heart: so shalt thou find favour and good understanding in the sight of God and man. *Proverbs 3:3-4*

Confess

Because I bind myself to mercy and truth and keep them in my heart, I have favor and good understanding with God and with man.

Wisdom

Trust in the Lord with all thine heart; and lean not unto thine own understanding. In all thy ways acknowledge him, and he shall direct thy paths. *Proverbs 3:5-6*

Confess

I trust in the Lord with all my heart, acknowledge Him in all my ways, and He directs my path.

51

Health

Be not wise in thine own eyes: fear the Lord, and depart from evil. It shall be health to thy navel, and marrow to thy bones.

Proverbs 3:7-8

Confess

I will not be wise in my own eyes. I honor the Lord and His commandments. I depart from evil and it brings health to my body.

Prosperous Life

Honour the Lord with thy substance, and with the first-fruits of all thine increase: so shall thy barns be filled with plenty, and thy presses shall burst out with new wine.

Proverbs 3:9-10

Confess

By giving of my increase to the Lord's work, I honor Him, and He blesses me with abundance in all that I do.

Protection

My son, let not them depart from thine eyes: keep sound wisdom and discretion: so shall they be life unto thy soul, and grace to thy neck. Then shalt thou walk in thy way safely, and thy foot shall not stumble. When thou liest down, thou shalt not be afraid: yea, thou shalt lie down, and thy sleep shall be sweet.

Proverbs 3:21-24

Confess

I keep sound wisdom and discretion, for they are life to my soul and beauty to my body. Because I keep common sense and discernment, I walk in safety and I do not stumble. I am not anxious or afraid to sleep; my sleep is sweet.

Relationships

Withhold not good from them to whom it is due, when it is in the power of thine hand to do it. Say not unto thy neighbour, Go, and come again, and to morrow I will give; when thou hast it by thee. Devise not evil against thy neighbour, seeing he dwelleth securely by thee.

Proverbs 3:27-29

Confess

When I have the power to do good things for others who deserve it, I do it. When I owe something, I pay it right away.

> Proverbs 4

Wisdom

Wisdom is the principal thing; therefore get wisdom: and with all thy getting get understanding. Exalt her, and she shall promote thee: she shall bring thee to honour, when thou dost embrace her.

Proverbs 4:7-8

Confess

I have embraced wisdom and it promotes and brings me to a position of honor.

Relationships

Enter not into the path of the wicked, and go not in the way of evil men. Avoid it, pass not by it, turn from it, and pass away. *Proverbs 4:14-15*

Confess

I avoid the path of the wicked.

Success

But the path of the just is as the shining light, that shineth more and more unto the perfect day. *Proverbs 4:18*

Confess

Because I am righteous through Christ, my path is like a shining light and my future is bright.

Health

My son, attend to my words; incline thine ear unto my sayings. Let them not depart from thine eyes; keep them in the midst of thine heart. For they are life unto those that find them, and health to all their flesh.

Proverbs 4:20-22

Confess

I read and meditate on the Word of the Lord. It is life to me and brings health to my body.

Wisdom

Keep thy heart with all diligence; for out of it are the issues of life. *Proverbs 4:23*

Confess

I guard my heart from evil, for my heart determines the way of my life.

> Proverbs 5

Success

And thou mourn at the last, when thy flesh and thy body are consumed, and say, How have I hated instruction, and my heart despised reproof; and have not obeyed the voice of my teachers, nor inclined mine ear to them that instructed me! *Proverbs 5:11-13*

Confess

I love instruction and receive reproof. I obey the voice of my teachers.

> Proverbs 6

Prosperous Life

Go to the ant, thou sluggard; consider her ways, and be wise: which having no guide, overseer, or ruler, provideth her meat in the summer, and gathereth her food in the harvest. *Proverbs 6: 6-8*

Confess

I am wise to make plans and provision for my future.

Success

My son, keep thy father's commandment, and forsake not the law of thy mother: bind them continually upon thine heart, and tie them about thy neck. When thou goest, it shall lead thee; when thou sleepest, it shall keep thee; and when thou awakest, it shall talk with thee.   *Proverbs 6:20-22*

Confess

The teachings of my parents lead me as I go. They keep me when I sleep, and when I awake, they speak to me.

> Proverbs 7

Success

My son, keep my words, and lay up my commandments with thee. Keep my commandments, and live; and my law as the apple of thine eye.   *Proverbs 7:1-2*

Confess

I keep God's commandments and live in success. The Word of God is the apple of my eye.

> Proverbs 8

Wisdom

For my mouth shall speak truth; and wickedness is an abomination to my lips. All the words of my mouth are in

righteousness; there is nothing froward or perverse in them. *Proverbs 8:7-8*

Confess

I speak words of truth. Doing wrong is detestable to me.

Success

I wisdom dwell with prudence, and find out knowledge of witty inventions. *Proverbs 8:12*

Confess

The wisdom of God gives me good judgment and knowledge of creative and witty inventions.

Favor

Blessed is the man that heareth me [wisdom], watching daily at my gates, waiting at the posts of my doors. For whoso findeth me findeth life, and shall obtain favour of the Lord. *Proverbs 8:34-35*

Confess

Daily, I listen and seek God's wisdom. When I find it, I've found life and the favor of the Lord.

> Proverbs 9

Relationships

He that reproveth a scorner getteth to himself shame: and he that rebuketh a wicked man getteth himself a blot.

57

Reprove not a scorner, lest he hate thee: rebuke a wise man, and he will love thee. *Proverbs 9:7-8*

Confess

I will not argue with someone who mocks me, because it will do no good, but I can reason with a wise person; they will appreciate it.

Health

The fear of the Lord is the beginning of wisdom: and the knowledge of the holy is understanding. For by me thy days shall be multiplied, and the years of thy life shall be increased. *Proverbs 9:10-11*

Confess

I honor the Lord and receive wisdom; knowledge of Him gives me understanding. By Him my days are multiplied and years are added to my life.

> Proverbs 10

Prosperous Life

He becometh poor that dealeth with a slack hand: but the hand of the diligent maketh rich. *Proverbs 10:4*

Confess

I am diligent and it makes me rich.

Prosperous Life

The blessing of the Lord, it maketh rich, and he addeth no sorrow with it.   *Proverbs 10:22*

Confess

The blessing of the Lord makes me rich and adds no sorrow with it.

> Proverbs 11

Wisdom

The integrity of the upright shall guide them: but the perverseness of transgressors shall destroy them.

Proverbs 11:3

Confess

My integrity guides me and keeps me.

Relationships

A talebearer revealeth secrets: but he that is of a faithful spirit concealeth the matter.   *Proverbs 11:13*

Confess

I refuse to gossip. I am of a faithful spirit and I keep the confidence of a friend.

Relationships

The merciful man doeth good to his own soul: but he that is cruel troubleth his own flesh.   *Proverbs 11:17*

Confess

I am merciful and kind to others and my deeds return to bless me.

> Proverbs 12

Favor

A good man obtaineth favour of the Lord: but a man of wicked devices will he condemn. *Proverbs 12:2*

Confess

Because I am truthful and try to do what's right instead of being manipulative, I receive favor from the Lord.

Success

A man shall be satisfied with good by the fruit of his mouth: and the recompence of a man's hands shall be rendered unto him. *Proverbs 12:14*

Confess

The good work of my hands will come back to me.

Protection

There shall no evil happen to the just: but the wicked shall be filled with mischief. *Proverbs 12:21*

Confess

No evil shall happen to me.

Wisdom

Lying lips are abomination to the Lord: but they that deal
truly are his delight. *Proverbs 12:22*

Confess
The Lord delights in me because I speak the truth.

> Proverbs 13

Wisdom

A man shall eat good by the fruit of his mouth: but the
soul of the transgressors shall eat violence. He that
keepeth his mouth keepeth his life: but he that openeth
wide his lips shall have destruction. *Proverbs 13:2-3*

Confess
By the words I speak, I enjoy many good things. I control
what I say and it brings me a long life!

Success

Wealth gotten by vanity shall be diminished: but he that
gathereth by labour shall increase. *Proverbs 13:11*

Confess
I work hard and honestly and my wealth grows and
becomes great.

Relationships

He that spareth his rod hateth his son: but he that loveth
him chasteneth him betimes. *Proverbs 13:24*

Confess

I receive discipline from my parents. I know that because they correct me, they love me and care about my future.

> Proverbs 14

Relationships

Go from the presence of a foolish man, when thou perceivest not in him the lips of knowledge.

Proverbs 14:7

Confess

I spend little time with people who talk foolishly.

Wisdom

The wisdom of the prudent is to understand his way: but the folly of fools is deceit.　　　*Proverbs 14:8*

Confess

I walk in the wisdom of God and watch my actions at all times.

Favor

Fools make a mock at sin: but among the righteous there is favour.　　　*Proverbs 14:9*

Confess

Fools may laugh about their sin, but because I am right-eous, I have favor.

Wisdom

A wise man feareth, and departeth from evil: but the fool
rageth, and is confident.   *Proverbs 14:16*

Confess

I honor the Lord and leave evil situations.

Protection

In the fear of the Lord is strong confidence: and his children shall have a place of refuge.   *Proverbs 14:26*

Confess

I have strong confidence in the Lord and in Him I always
have a place of refuge.

> Proverbs 15

Success

All the days of the afflicted are evil: but he that is of a
merry heart hath a continual feast.   *Proverbs 15:15*

Confess

Even if trouble comes, I have a cheerful countenance and
enjoy life.

Success

A man hath joy by the answer of his mouth: and a word
spoken in due season, how good is it!   *Proverbs 15:23*

Confess

The answers I give bring me joy. I speak the right words at the right time.

Wisdom

The heart of the righteous studieth to answer: but the mouth of the wicked poureth out evil things.

Proverbs 15:28

Confess

I study so I can answer wisely.

Success

The fear of the Lord is the instruction of wisdom; and before honour is humility.   *Proverbs 15:33*

Confess

I have wisdom because I honor the Lord, and I receive honor because I walk in humility.

> Proverbs 16

Success

Commit thy works unto the Lord, and thy thoughts shall be established.   *Proverbs 16:3*

Confess

My work is committed to God, my thoughts are established, and my plans succeed.

Protection

When a man's ways please the Lord, he maketh even his enemies to be at peace with him.   *Proverbs 16:7*

Confess

My ways please the Lord. He makes even my enemies to be at peace with me.

Wisdom

Pride goeth before destruction, and an haughty spirit before a fall. Better it is to be of an humble spirit with the lowly, than to divide the spoil with the proud.

Proverbs 16:18-19

Confess

Because I refuse to be full of pride, I avoid making mistakes. I am of a humble spirit and I honor the Lord.

Health

Pleasant words are as an honeycomb, sweet to the soul, and health to the bones.   *Proverbs 16:24*

Confess

I speak pleasant words that are as a honeycomb, sweet to the mind and healing to my body.

Relationships

An ungodly man diggeth up evil: and in his lips there is as a burning fire. A froward man soweth strife: and a whisperer separateth chief friends.   *Proverbs 16:27-28*

Confess

I refuse to cause strife or gossip about my friends.

Wisdom

He that is slow to anger is better than the mighty; and he that ruleth his spirit than he that taketh a city.

Proverbs 16:32

Confess

I have self-control, I am slow to anger, and I rule my own spirit.

> Proverbs 17

Relationships

He that covereth a transgression seeketh love; but he that repeateth a matter separateth very friends.

Proverbs 17:9

Confess

I choose not to gossip about a matter but instead to walk in love and forgive.

Health

A merry heart doeth good like a medicine: but a broken spirit drieth the bones.　　　*Proverbs 17:22*

Confess

I have a happy countenance and it keeps me healthy and strong.

Wisdom

He that hath knowledge spareth his words: and a man of
understanding is of an excellent spirit. Even a fool, when he
holdeth his peace, is counted wise: and he that shutteth his
lips is esteemed a man of understanding.   *Proverbs 17:27-28*

Confess

I am a person with knowledge. I think about what I'm
going to say and only say what makes sense. I have an
excellent spirit and I am a person of understanding.

> Proverbs 18

Protection

The name of the Lord is a strong tower: the righteous
runneth into it, and is safe.   *Proverbs 18:10*

Confess

God's name is a strong tower; I run into it and I am safe.

Favor

A man's gift maketh room for him, and bringeth him
before great men.   *Proverbs 18:16*

Confess

My gift makes room for me and brings me before great men.

Relationships

He that is first in his own cause seemeth just; but his
neighbour cometh and searcheth him.   *Proverbs 18:17*

Confess

I have wisdom and hear both sides of an argument before
I decide who is right.

Wisdom

Death and life are in the power of the tongue: and they
that love it shall eat the fruit thereof.   *Proverbs 18:21*

Confess

I speak life to my situations by speaking the Word of God
concerning them.

Relationships

A man that hath friends must shew himself friendly: and
there is a friend that sticketh closer than a brother.

Proverbs 18:24

Confess

I demonstrate friendliness; therefore, I have friends that
stick by me like family.

> Proverbs 19

Prosperous Life

He that getteth wisdom loveth his own soul: he that
keepeth understanding shall find good.   *Proverbs 19:8*

Confess

I work to get wisdom because I love my own soul; I keep
understanding and prosper.

Relationships

The discretion of a man deferreth his anger; and it is his glory to pass over a transgression.   *Proverbs 19:11*

Confess

I use self-control to keep my emotions in check and I earn respect by overlooking offenses.

Prosperous Life

Slothfulness casteth into a deep sleep; and an idle soul shall suffer hunger.   *Proverbs 19:15*

Confess

I am diligent to do my work and be alert; I will always have plenty.

Relationships

He that hath pity upon the poor lendeth unto the Lord; and that which he hath given will he pay him again.

Proverbs 19:17

Confess

I give to those who cannot pay me back, but the Lord repays me with great blessings.

Wisdom

Hear counsel, and receive instruction, that thou mayest be wise in thy latter end.   *Proverbs 19:20*

Confess

I accept correction. It makes me wise in times to come.

Success

There are many devices in a man's heart; nevertheless the counsel of the Lord, that shall stand.   *Proverbs 19:21*

Confess

I may have many ideas, but it is the Lord's purpose for me that will stand.

> Proverbs 20

Wisdom

Wine is a mocker, strong drink is raging: and whosoever is deceived thereby is not wise.   *Proverbs 20:1*

Confess

Wine is a mocker and strong drink is raging. I refuse to be led astray by them.

Success

Even a child is known by his doings, whether his work be pure, and whether it be right.   *Proverbs 20:11*

Confess

I am known by my doings, that my work is pure and right.

Success

Every purpose is established by counsel: and with good advice make war.   *Proverbs 20:18*

Confess
Before I make any big decisions, I seek out godly counsel;
and so my purposes are established and successful.

Relationships

He that goeth about as a talebearer revealeth secrets:
therefore meddle not with him that flattereth with his lips.

Proverbs 20:19

Confess
I refuse to be someone who betrays the confidence of
others and I avoid those who gossip.

Relationships

Say not thou, I will recompense evil; but wait on the Lord,
and he shall save thee.   *Proverbs 20:22*

Confess
I am not vindictive. I wait on the Lord and He delivers me.

> Proverbs 21

Prosperous Life

The thoughts of the diligent tend only to plenteousness;
but of every one that is hasty only to want.

Proverbs 21:5

Confess
I am diligent. I think of—and carefully plan for—the mani-
festation of abundance in my life.

Prosperous Life

There is treasure to be desired and oil in the dwelling of the wise; but a foolish man spendeth it up.   *Proverbs 21:20*

Confess

When it comes to money, I use the wisdom of God and have great treasure.

Success

He that followeth after righteousness and mercy findeth life, righteousness, and honour.   *Proverbs 21:21*

Confess

I seek after and crave righteousness and mercy, which cause me to experience honor and the true meaning of living a successful life in the kingdom of God.

Success

There is no wisdom nor understanding nor counsel against the Lord.   *Proverbs 21:30*

Confess

The Lord is for me; and there is no human wisdom or understanding or counsel that can prevail against Him.

> Proverbs 22

Success

By humility and the fear of the Lord are riches, and honour, and life.   *Proverbs 22:4*

72

Confess

I reverently fear the Lord and I am experiencing riches
and honor in my life.

Prosperous Life

He that hath a bountiful eye shall be blessed; for he giveth
of his bread to the poor.   *Proverbs 22:9*

Confess

I am generous and blessed by the Lord because I give to
the poor.

Relationships

Cast out the scorner, and contention shall go out; yea,
strife and reproach shall cease.   *Proverbs 22:10*

Confess

I avoid mockers and scorners. When they are gone, fight-
ing and quarreling stops.

Wisdom

Foolishness is bound in the heart of a child; but the rod of
correction shall drive it far from him.   *Proverbs 22:15*

Confess

I receive discipline because it drives foolishness from
my heart.

Relationships

Make no friendship with an angry man; and with a furious
man thou shalt not go: lest thou learn his ways, and get a
snare to thy soul.   *Proverbs 22:24-25*

73

iGod

Wisdom From Proverbs

Confess

I avoid angry and hot-tempered people so that I do not become like them.

Success

Seest thou a man diligent in his business? he shall stand before kings; he shall not stand before mean men.

Proverbs 22:29

Confess

I am diligent and skillful in my business (school) and it brings me before great leaders.

> Proverbs 23

Success

For as he thinketh in his heart, so is he: Eat and drink, saith he to thee; but his heart is not with thee.

Proverbs 23:7

Confess

In my heart, I believe I am successful; therefore I am.

Success

Let not thine heart envy sinners: but be thou in the fear of the Lord all the day long. For surely there is an end; and thine expectation shall not be cut off.

Proverbs 23:17-18

Confess

I refuse to envy others. Instead, I honor the Lord at all times. I know He has a good plan for my life and my hope is secure.

> Proverbs 24

Prosperous Life

Through wisdom is an house builded; and by understanding it is established: and by knowledge shall the chambers be filled with all precious and pleasant riches.

Proverbs 24:3-4

Confess

By wisdom I build my life. By good sense I establish my life. By knowledge I fill my life with precious and great riches.

Relationships

If thou forbear to deliver them that are drawn unto death, and those that are ready to be slain; if thou sayest, Behold, we knew it not; doth not he that pondereth the heart consider it? and he that keepeth thy soul, doth not he know it? and shall not he render to every man according to his works?

Proverbs 24:11-12

Confess

If someone is headed for great trouble, I will not ignore it. I will try to stop them. The Lord knows my heart and will reward me for helping others.

75

Protection

For a just man falleth seven times, and riseth up again: but the wicked shall fall into mischief. *Proverbs 24:16*

Confess

If I fall, I get up immediately.

Relationships

Rejoice not when thine enemy falleth, and let not thine heart be glad when he stumbleth: lest the Lord see it, and it displease him, and he turn away his wrath from him.

Proverbs 24:17-18

Confess

I refuse to rejoice when my enemies fall because it does not please the Lord.

> Proverbs 25

Relationships

Debate thy cause with thy neighbour himself; and discover not a secret to another: lest he that heareth it put thee to shame, and thine infamy turn not away.

Proverbs 25:9-10

Confess

When talking with others, I refuse to betray the confidence of a friend. In that way, I keep my good reputation and my friend.

76

Success

A word fitly spoken is like apples of gold in pictures of silver. *Proverbs 25:11*

Confess

I speak words in due season to people around me and it blesses everyone.

Relationships

By long forbearing is a prince persuaded, and a soft tongue breaketh the bone. *Proverbs 25:15*

Confess

In the midst of chaos, I am calm; and my soft speech breaks down stubborn resistance.

Relationships

If thine enemy be hungry, give him bread to eat; and if he be thirsty, give him water to drink: for thou shalt heap coals of fire upon his head, and the Lord shall reward thee. *Proverbs 25:21-22*

Confess

I am generous towards my enemies. I feed them if they are hungry and give them a drink if they are thirsty, and God rewards me!

Protection

He that hath no rule over his own spirit is like a city that is broken down, and without walls. *Proverbs 25:28*

Confess

I exercise self-control over my own desires and I am
protected from trouble.

> Proverbs 26

Relationships

Answer not a fool according to his folly, lest thou also be
like unto him. *Proverbs 26:4*

Confess

I avoid foolish conversations with foolish people, so that I
do not become as a fool myself.

Wisdom

He that passeth by, and meddleth with strife belonging
not to him, is like one that taketh a dog by the ears.

Proverbs 26:17

Confess

I avoid strife. I only attend to my business.

Relationships

Whoso diggeth a pit shall fall therein: and he that rolleth a
stone, it will return upon him. *Proverbs 26:27*

Confess

Any traps set for me will trap the people who set them.

> Proverbs 27

Wisdom

Boast not thyself of to morrow; for thou knowest not
what a day may bring forth. Let another man praise thee,
and not thine own mouth; a stranger, and not thine own
lips.   *Proverbs 27:1-2*

Confess

I refuse to boast about my future. I let others praise me
instead of myself.

Protection

A prudent man foreseeth the evil, and hideth himself; but
the simple pass on, and are punished.   *Proverbs 27:12*

Confess

I am discerning and smart. I foresee evil and take precau-
tions to avoid it.

Relationships

He that blesseth his friend with a loud voice, rising early
in the morning, it shall be counted a curse to him.

Proverbs 27:14

Confess

I make sure that I am not loud and obnoxious early in the
morning; otherwise, no one will like me.

Relationships

Iron sharpeneth iron; so a man sharpeneth the countenance of his friend.   *Proverbs 27:17*

Confess

As iron sharpens iron, I sharpen the countenance of my friends.

Success

Be thou diligent to know the state of thy flocks, and look well to thy herds. For riches are not for ever: and doth the crown endure to every generation?   *Proverbs 27:23-24*

Confess

I am diligent to know the state of my affairs.
Inheritances and riches do not last forever with no one watching over them.

> Proverbs 28

Success

The wicked flee when no man pursueth: but the righteous are bold as a lion.   *Proverbs 28:1*

Confess

I am the righteousness of God and as bold as a lion.

Wisdom

Evil men understand not judgment: but they that seek the Lord understand all things.   *Proverbs 28:5*

Confess

I seek the Lord's counsel and He helps me to understand all things.

Relationships

Whoso keepeth the law is a wise son: but he that is a companion of riotous men shameth his father.

Proverbs 28:7

Confess

I keep the law of the land and make my parent(s) proud.

Favor

He that covereth his sins shall not prosper: but whoso confesseth and forsaketh them shall have mercy.

Proverbs 28:13

Confess

I prosper and receive mercy because I confess and renounce my mistakes.

Prosperous Life

A faithful man shall abound with blessings: but he that maketh haste to be rich shall not be innocent.

Proverbs 28:20

Confess

I avoid get-rich-quick schemes. I am a faithful person and I abound with blessings.

81

Prosperous Life

He that is of a proud heart stirreth up strife: but he that
putteth his trust in the Lord shall be made fat.

Proverbs 28:25

Confess

I refuse to be greedy. My trust is in the Lord, and He prospers me.

> Proverbs 29

Success

When the righteous are in authority, the people rejoice:
but when the wicked beareth rule, the people mourn.

Proverbs 29:2

Confess

I support righteous men and women in authority, for it is
then that the people rejoice.

Wisdom

A fool uttereth all his mind: but a wise man keepeth it in
till afterwards.   *Proverbs 29:11*

Confess

I refuse to speak whatever pops into my mind. I wait and
determine what to say when it's appropriate.

Success

Where there is no vision, the people perish: but he that keepeth the law, happy is he. *Proverbs 29:18*

Confess

I seek God's will for my life and vision for my future so that I can achieve great things. I will not perish.

> Proverbs 30

Protection

Every word of God is pure: he is a shield unto them that put their trust in him. *Proverbs 30:5*

Confess

My trust is in God; therefore, He is my shield.

Relationships

If thou hast done foolishly in lifting up thyself, or if thou hast thought evil, lay thine hand upon thy mouth.

Proverbs 30:32

Confess

I refuse to exalt myself or plan evil, because it is shameful.

> Proverbs 31

Wisdom

Give not thy strength unto women, nor thy ways to that which destroyeth kings.   *Proverbs 31:3*

Confess

I do not give myself to habits or things that will destroy my influence or my future.

Wisdom

Open thy mouth for the dumb in the cause of all such as are appointed to destruction. Open thy mouth, judge righteously, and plead the cause of the poor and needy.

Proverbs 31:8-9

Confess

I help others who are in need.

> The Seven Success Practices for Students

1. **S**tudy and attend school (class) regularly.
   Practice and cultivate and meditate upon these duties; throw yourself wholly into them (as your ministry) so that your progress may be evident to everybody....
   I Timothy 4:15 AMP

2. **T**rust in the Lord.
   Trust in the Lord with all thine heart; and lean not unto thine own understanding. In all thy ways acknowledge him, and he shall direct thy paths.   *Proverbs 3: 5-6*

3. **U**se time wisely.
   To everything there is a season, and a time for every matter or purpose under heaven.   *Ecclesiastes 3:1 AMP*

4. **D**etermine to succeed.
   Forgetting what lies behind and straining forward to what lies ahead, I press on toward the goal to win.
   Philippians 3:13-14 AMP

5. **E**liminate ungodly friendships.
   Do not be so deceived and misled! Evil companion-ships (communion, associations) corrupt and deprave

85

good manners and morals and character.

1 Corinthians 15:33 AMP

6. **N**avigate successfully through temporary interruptions.

There hath no temptation taken you but such as is common to man: but God is faithful, who will not suffer you to be tempted above that ye are able; but will with the temptation also make a way to escape, that you may be able to bear it.

1 Corinthians 10:13

7. **T**riumph in every situation.

Now thanks be unto God, which always causeth us to triumph in Christ, and maketh manifest the savour of his knowledge by us in every place.

2 Corinthians 2:14

> Prayer of Salvation

God loves you—no matter who you are, no matter what your past. God loves you so much that He gave His one and only begotten Son for you. The Bible tells us that "whoever believes in him shall not perish but have eternal life" (John 3:16 NIV). Jesus laid down His life and rose again so that we could spend eternity with Him in heaven and experience His absolute best on earth. If you would like to receive Jesus into your life, say the following prayer out loud and mean it from your heart:

Heavenly Father, I come to You admitting that I am a sinner. Right now, I choose to turn away from sin, and I ask You to cleanse me of all unrighteousness. I believe that Your Son, Jesus, died on the cross to take away my sins. I also believe that He rose again from the dead so that I might be forgiven of my sins and made righteous through faith in Him. I call upon the name of Jesus Christ to be the Savior and Lord of my life. Jesus, I choose to follow You and ask that You fill me with the power of the Holy Spirit. I declare that right now I am a child of God. I am free from sin and full of the righteousness of God. I am saved in Jesus' name. Amen.

If you prayed this prayer to receive Jesus Christ as your Savior for the first time, please contact us on the web at **www.harrisonhouse.com** to receive a free book.

Or you may write to us at
Harrison House
P.O. Box 35035
Tulsa, Oklahoma 74153

Please visit our website for a complete listing of all our books: **www.harrisonhouse.com**

> About the Author

Dr. Josie Washington Carr has a love for God and a love for learning. She currently serves as an executive director of education. Throughout her twenty plus years in education, Dr. Carr has served as a teacher, principal, and special education coordinator.

Dr. Carr was formally educated at Texas Southern University in Houston, Texas. She holds an undergraduate degree in physical education, two masters degrees in special education and mid-management, and a doctorate in educational leadership.

Dr. Carr enjoys fulfilling her purpose in life through ministry and education, spending time with her family, and helping others to achieve their highest potential. She is the wife of Dr. Stanley Carr and the proud mother of Jarvis and Jakia Carr.

To contact Dr. Josie Carr,
please write to:
P.O. Box 672514
Houston, Texas 77267
jocarrmd@yahoo.com